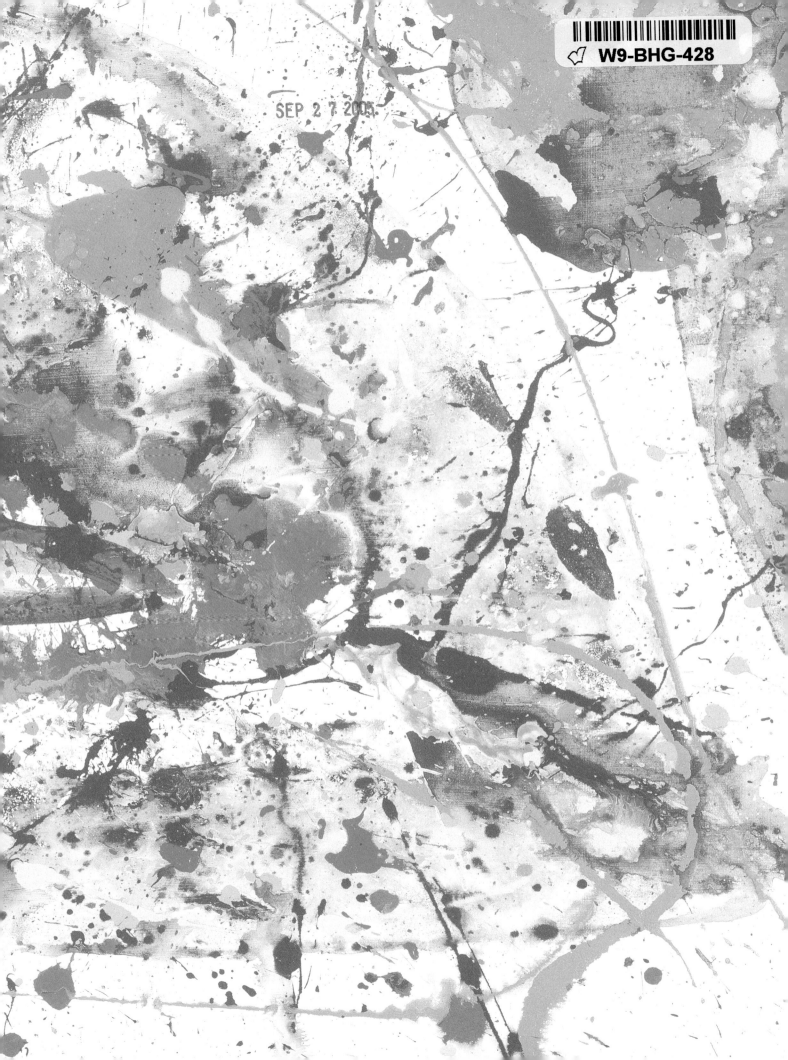

SAM FRANCIS

SAM FRANCIS

WITH CONTRIBUTIONS BY

Jerry Aistrip

Daniel Cytron

Nico Delaive

André Emmerich

Sam Francis

Nancy Mozur

George Page

Jeff Perkins

Robert Shapazian

Douglas Shields

Martin Sosin

EDITED BY

Marian Winsryg

Color Is the Essence of It All

MARTIN SOSIN · SANTA MONICA, CALIFORNIA · 2003

Publisher: Martin Sosin, 211 California Avenue #401,
Santa Monica, California 90403, Telephone (310) 393-6032

Special thanks to:
Jerry Aistrip
Debra Burchette-Lere
Daniel Cytron
Nico Delaive
André Emmerich
Nancy Mozur
George Page
Jeff Perkins
Robert Shapazian
Douglas Shields

Sam Francis: Color Is the Essence of It All is published in conjunction with
an exhibition of the same name held at Santa Monica College, Santa
Monica, California, October 11 through December 4, 2003.

Editor & Curator: Marian Winsryg
Book Designers: Carol Ring and Don Girard
Photographer: Susan Einstein
Printer: Costello Brothers, Alhambra, Calif.
Bookbinder: Roswell Bookbinding, Phoenix, Ariz.

This catalogue is made in an edition of 2,500 copies.

ISBN 0-9744072-0-8

Cover: Detail of an untitled lithograph (SF 340)

Contents

INTRODUCTION

WORKING IN THE DARK

Robert Shapazian

*I*n the course of my task as director of the book publishing company owned by Sam Francis, he and I would speak together frequently. Every time I heard his voice, my spirit would jump, for I knew I was about to have another inspiring conversation with my dear friend, a conversation full of great humor, great ideas, enthusiasm, affection, dreaming, and passion for everything we discussed. When he called one summer afternoon, his voice was unusually soft and cautious, as though he were going to tell me a secret. "Robert, you know, in a few days I'll be getting some drawings that have been in storage in my Tokyo studio for years. They're very special. Very dark. Black drawings. You know, things that I haven't shown much, and that people don't know very well, that they don't understand. They're very personal and important to me. I want you to see them."

Sam was inviting me to see work that he considered intensely private and deeply interior. When we viewed the drawings, I found them mysterious and full of paradox. Here were dark studies in pools of black ink made by this supreme master of brilliant color, a man who searched the world for rare pigments, who ground them like an alchemist, who created beautiful shades that were uniquely his. What were these dark works? Why the decision to pull back from color into this black essence? My first reaction was puzzled disappointment.

As I looked at the paintings, however, what my rational mind questioned, my feelings and intuition did not. Yes, they were black designs on white paper, with infrequent touches of color. But each was exuberant and gorgeous, with all the intensity and energy that I associated with Sam's full spectrum of color. My eyes saw black, but I felt a complete range of brilliance as well as darkness. Even the most densely painted studies contained great light and clarity. My knowledge of Sam's coloristic works gave me insight into these dark drawings. Each mode revealed something about the other.

So these works were not less, because of their insistence on black. They were, nevertheless, a conspicuous renunciation of the variety of color and everything unique to it. In these monochromes, Sam seemed to retreat from, let us say, the florid beauty of the world into an extremely interior place of essence and concentration. We might call it the place of in-sight. I understood this after discovering these lines written by him in one of his many notebooks:

Insight is in the dark

All insights are dark

What does this mean? Insight grows out of darkness, out of prior obscurity. Insight rises from depth toward illumination. But insight also increases depth and profundity, opening a new terrain of mystery. One can go on and on, trying to unravel this paradox about the eternal and creative relationship between opposites of all kinds. Sam believed the truth of this paradox completely.

Thinking more about his work, I realized that black images occur throughout his career. They are a constant, like the essential interior Being of the artist himself. Set against them is the abundant variety of all the coloristic works, which, as they change in shape and hue, always relate to the dark constant. This is true even during the early 1950s, when Sam made the large paintings that resemble a translucent and airy atmosphere of uniform white, or blue, or light orange. At the same, he was making small works on paper in clotted black, but identical to the colored canvases in the overall application of pigment. The small studies actually anticipate both the masses of black paint and large areas of high color that dominate the large paintings several years later.

In the artist's notebooks, we find other paradoxical statements about the relationship of darkness to the appearance of lightness and air:

> *an increase in light*
> *gives an increase in darkness*
> *This painting gets more airy as it gets darker*
> *Color is born of the interpenetration of light*
> *And dark.*

> *Working in the Dark*

The relationship is clear: darkness is a creative companion to its opposite; the spareness of black engenders the abundant beauty of colors. Wholeness is the willingness to do it all.

I am attempting to tell you something about the special significance of "working in the dark," or "working with the dark," as it relates to the deepest artistic and personal exploration of Sam Francis. Thinking about him, I remembered that nearly all of his self-portraits are painted, etched, or lithographed in black inks. A few exist in monochromatic red or blue, but their solid color is like the singularity of black. This is a very simple but clear point: For Sam Francis, black is the material and the tool to examine, explore, and fashion the image of himself.

This is especially apparent in the large group of graphic self-portraits he made during the 1970s that he called "Anima Prints." At the time, Sam was engaged in Jungian analysis, which provided concepts to aid his exploration of his personal and artistic being. In Jungian theory, the anima is the feminine principle that men must explore in order to augment their primary and external male persona. In men, the anima is hidden, internal, unconscious. It is sometimes called the "not-I." Associated with emotion, intuition, and creativity, it resides in womb-like and pregnant interior darkness. Anima is the archetype of life itself. Most important, Jung defined it as a psychic image. In this regard, two quotes from the notebooks of Sam Francis are especially relevant:

> *My consciousness is an image. Everything of which I am conscious is image.*
> *All my experience is psychic.*

The Anima Prints are, therefore, an index, or guide, to the relationship Sam Francis forged between monochromatic black, the darkness of the hidden self, and the creation of his psychic and visual image. It is no wonder that studies in black exist throughout his career, always penetrating, examining, and prefiguring ideas and forms that later blossom into full color, form, and scale.

The idea of relationship was always crucial to Sam: the relationship between dark and light, soul and matter, life and death, and an infinity of possible combinations. As he wrote in his notebooks, "Depth of All." For him, relations are never static, fixed, or resolved. Instead, they are potent, even chaotic, and pregnant with an infinite deepness of searching, possibility, and creativity.

> *Why do we say "shades" of colors?*
> *— shadows of colors —*
> *Who has seen pure white?*

His preferred term "shadow" means the interplay and integration of light and dark, of substance and immateriality. But "shadow" also means a reflection—a thing seeing itself. Were we discussing this with Sam Francis, I know he would push our definition of "reflection" to include the meanings of thought, introspection, and questioning. So, we are again in that world so characteristic of him, where everything is elusive yet exuberantly full. There is no pure white, no pure black. They are mixed and reciprocal, containing the whole spectrum of color and possibility. At the beginning of my remarks, I said that his black drawings seemed to me just as florid and gorgeous as his works in color. When you can experience this for yourself, you experience something essential about Sam's great creativity: his ability to express in a work of art his most deep, elusive, and mysterious perceptions of himself and reality.

We have heard many times the saying that it takes courage to be creative. Why is this? Because creation is the making of something out of nothing, where nothing existed before. It is "Working in the Dark." One must have fearlessness and self-confidence to work in the dark, for one is most vulnerable there. But great humility, great trust, and an abiding love of creation, in all its aspects, also must be present in anyone who gives himself entirely to the deepest creative life. I can personally attest, this is absolutely the kind of man that Sam Francis was.

3

THE MAKING OF THE DAVIS, FISCHER, SOSIN FAMILIES SAM FRANCIS ART COLLECTION, 1962 TO 1994

Martin Sosin

*A*s a new member of the California Bar, I started to make the rounds as a rubber chicken professional speaker to widen my availability as a CPA/tax lawyer. I was invited to the Santa Monica Bar Association luncheon meeting, at the end of which I was approached by one of the attendees, Bill Elliot. He was a patent lawyer and told me he had a friend, a local artist, who needed my talents. We scheduled a meeting for shortly thereafter at Sam's Venice, California, Main Street storefront address, i.e., 1378 Main Street, Venice, California. This was in the early part of 1962.

We arrived at Sam's studio in the early afternoon. Sam was resting on a bed that he usually had in all his studios. He claimed that he dreamed often, which gave rise to the colorful images that he painted.

We were introduced and I was amazed. I thought I was looking in a mirror. Sam and I were so much alike—we both were 5' 6" tall, robust in build, about 160 pounds, ruddy complexion, brown hair, blue eyes. As it turned out, we were about the same age; Sam was born in 1923 and I was born in 1922. It was uncanny.

Sam Francis: "Marty, Bill thinks I need a guy like you to handle my business affairs. How shall we handle this new relationship? I want you to do anything you believe will help me financially and the business part of my painting activities. I must remind you. I hate paperwork."

Marty Sosin: "I must remind you—my life's blood is paperwork."

Sam Francis: "Alright, alright. Do what you must, just pass the material by me as I'm interested in all those things and I'll sign whatever I must just to humor you. Don't keep any records that most lawyers do, and I'll give you paintings in exchange for your services. From time to time, we'll sit down in my studio and you can pick whatever paintings you want for your services. No restrictions!"

Sam was completely a right-brained artist and I was completely a left-brained businessman. We were a perfect match, which probably accounts for our long relationship. It turns out that I was Sam's alter ego. If he had a favorite masseur, he arranged for me to get massages. Sam was into homeopathic medicine, so if I needed medical treatment, Sam arranged for me to see a homeopathic practitioner. Sam was devoted to Jungian psychiatry and was being treated by Jack Kirsch, a Jungian, so I had to also be treated by him, and on and on.

So that started my thirty-three-year career as Sam's alter ego and the creation of the Davis, Fischer, Sosin Families Sam Francis Art Collection.

SAM AND MARTY: THE COLLECTION

Robert Shapazian

Among his many creative projects, Sam Francis established a book publishing company, the Lapis Press, and I was fortunate enough to work there, and ultimately to direct it, for eight years—until Sam's death in 1994.

The first time I met Sam was at my job interview. In a fashion typical of him, we talked, philosophized, and laughed a lot, and I was forcefully introduced to his mesmerizing charm, his enormously affectionate spirit, and piercing blue eyes. Of course, by the end of the meeting, I was completely swept away and felt, as I still do, that I was the luckiest person in the world to have the chance to work with him.

As our meeting was just about to end, Sam pushed back his chair and got up to see me out. His parting words were, "Of course, you'll have to talk with Martin Sosin. He's my lawyer and handles all the details." With that, Sam looked analytically into the distance and telegraphed the impression that this Martin Sosin was definitely all-knowing and entrusted with the keys to the kingdom. In short, my meeting with him would be the acid test.

Sure enough, several days later, I went to see this Martin Sosin. He was seated behind a large desk, piled with papers, surrounded by tables piled with even more papers, folders, and legal-size yellow envelopes. He treated me matter-of-factly and asked piercing questions in a blunt but intriguingly dramatic way: who was I, what did I want, what could I do, and what was I expecting? In short, it was the third degree. But, I liked him immediately, because he conveyed his own version of the astuteness, warmth, and sense of creative possibility I felt with Sam. It was perfectly obvious how they could be such close friends and colleagues.

Over the years, I came to feel the greatest affection for Sam and Martin and, in so many instances, the names were mentioned together. Whenever there was a project at hand and its worldly problems to untangle, Marty was summoned and appeared immediately. Sam counted on his opinion and trust and he, in turn, was inspired and nurtured by the other's greatness of heart, spirit, and genius.

The collection of artworks by Sam, gathered by Martin Sosin over the long period of their friendship, bears the marks of this affection and appreciative relationship between them—truly one of brotherly love. Each work of art was a kind of token of it.

So, I invite the viewer to be attentive to this dialogue, for it resides in this collection and makes it unique.

SAM AND NANCY:
HER SHADOW KNEW HIM BEST

Nancy Mozur

My first meeting with Sam Francis in 1971 at Gemini GEL was a case of mistaken identity. Sam came in to make prints, and I immediately thought that he was Francis Bacon due to my mixed-up slide memorization techniques as a UCLA art undergraduate. Little did I know. We liked each other; he recognized my potential and enlisted me to work for him in the fall of that year. Ali Baba's door had just opened, as well as my own world.

For eighteen years as Litho Shop codirector and curator, I experienced Sam's artistic flow and the environment that was cultivated. It was quite an international brew that gathered over time at his studio. Dealers, museum directors, artists, and collectors from all over Europe, Japan, and America met to do business over a handshake, sitting around the shop table recounting anecdotes and awaiting the sight of Sam's latest works. There was a broader attitude toward art then, and I feel that it was a gift that Sam included all of us in the passion, respect, and knowledge that was generated.

Under his auspices we had free reign as long as our efforts served the creative process and the exploration of his own work. While there, we were privy to the production of lithographs, etchings, and monotypes, the cycles of painting, and the formation of Lapis Press books. In addition, he supported interest in wind energy (Wind Harvest Co.), Jungian psychology (resulting in the film *Matter of Heart*), and alternative medicine. The studio was also open to other endeavors involving such artists as Richard Diebenkorn, Walasse Ting, Judy Chicago, and Dorothea Tanning. This was an artist who went way beyond the focus of his individual commitment to painting.

Everyone who encountered Sam thought they knew him deeply. But I was left with the impression that he was very much a lone polestar with a multitude circling around him. Sometimes I felt that this propelled him to create. He would reveal different aspects to everyone, playing magus, trickster, seducer, and mentor. He had the courage in my eyes to fully live out his own light and dark nature, which at times was difficult for those close to him. And yet years later, Sam continues to be an enigma, defying the gravity of definition and deferring to the imaginative expression of color, whiteness, inner structure, and expansive space. Here lies the invitation to know him —as a vessel of something greater than his person.

6

SAM AND THE STONE

George Page

$\mathscr{A}$lthough it may be difficult to precisely define the genesis of Sam Francis's lifelong commitment to graphics, certainly his early years in Paris (1950–1952) must have been a strong influence. This was a period of great lithographic rejuvenation, thanks to Pablo Picasso's extended work with Paris lithographer Fernand Mourlot.

In America, the miniscule flame of lithography was beginning to glow a brilliant blue at the Tamarind Lithographic Workshop, which opened in 1963 and began to engage our leading artists in the challenge of this complicated and mysterious process. My personal path to lithography began at the Herron School of Art in Indianapolis, Indiana. I loved the physical presence of the stones and the excitement of drawing on the stones, calculating the etches, and watching as the image emerged with each pass of the leather roller. Fortunately, my mentor was Garo Z. Antreasian, the first master printer of Tamarind. After a year of teaching lithography, I came to Los Angeles and began printing professionally at Gemini Ltd. in 1965.

I first met Sam in July of 1971, when he was drawing a series of eleven color prints at Gemini GEL. Sam had already purchased a used lithographic press from Tamarind and had set up the press in his Santa Monica painting studio. I began work with Sam on March 19, 1973, and for twenty-two years printed 149 editions using the small, hand-operated press that he had originally purchased for fifteen hundred dollars.

Sam's approach to collaboration between artist and printer was generous and free of constraints. He wanted to have fun and experiment with every image, and I was encouraged to join in the fun and express my own intuition and ideas. Because of his great confidence and prodigious drawing skills, he was able to complete the drawings rather quickly. He would then carefully designate which plate was to be printed in yellow, blue, or red. The color proofing session that followed was an exciting, high-energy process that eventually led to the printed edition.

For several years Sam's painting studio was located within walking distance of the print shop, and this created a very dynamic interchange. The paintings directed a creative flow to the prints, and the prints directed experimental images to the paintings. We often editioned two versions of the same image. The first version was in full color, and the second version was printed in black with gray accents, which were tinted with red, green, and silver. These gray versions were primarily for Sam's enjoyment, as he loved the subtle layering of the saturated tones.

Working at the Litho Shop was a totally fulfilling artistic experience and has given me a great sense of accomplishment. I am very thankful to Sam Francis for allowing me to be a part of his journey.

THE IDEAL DEALER

André Emmerich

*M*y initial encounter with the work of Sam Francis was on my first trip to Paris after the war in the summer of 1953 while still a journalist. His work was in a group show of new art organized by the influential French critic Michel Tapié entitled *Un art autre (Another Kind of Art)*. On that same trip, I also saw one of his powerful paintings at the home of Darthea Speyer, who at that time was the cultural attaché for the United States embassy in Paris. She also organized Sam's first one-man show at the Galerie du Dragon in the heart of the Montparnasse section of Paris, a show whose spectacular success reverberated a year later.

My response to Sam's art was both immediate and profound. It stirred me deeply, and I found it exhilarating.

I returned to Paris in 1954, determined to be an art dealer and looking for artists to show in the gallery I planned to open in New York. But by that time, Sam had soared out of reach for a young would-be dealer without, as yet, even a location to call his own. But this did not diminish my growing admiration for Sam's new paintings, which I found more beautiful than ever.

It was not until 1968 that I was able to woo Sam away from the Pierre Matisse Gallery and install an exhibition of his new paintings in my 57th Street gallery the following year. This began a long, happy, and intensely personal relationship with Sam that lasted until his untimely passing in 1994. It was marked by my frequent trips to Santa Monica to visit his studio and plan his almost annual exhibitions.

Slowly, over the years, Sam and I grew closer in our personal friendship and in his trust in me as his dealer and in my eye. The latter actually proved to create its own problems for me. The more he valued my eye, the more he tended to want to hang on to paintings to which I responded particularly strongly. As a result, he often decided to keep them for himself rather than ship them to New York. The only leverage I had was to remind him that New York in those years was the very epicenter of the art world, the place where his exhibitions had to compete with the best new art being produced and where critical judgments were constantly being formed and reformed. I pointed out to him that it was for his own interest, even more than mine, that he put his best foot forward on 57th Street. The other way to loosen Sam's understandable grip on his best work was to plead and plead again the depths of my enthusiasm, which often moved him to let my favorite pictures come to New York.

In all our inevitably complex artist-dealer relationships, Sam always proved to be a generous and appreciative friend. That was why it was a continuing pleasure for me to go beyond what might be required from a dealer.

Thinking back on my association with Sam and his work, it is his infectious enthusiasm for the very act and art of painting that his work continues to radiate. To look at his pictures is to share the immense pleasure he obviously had in the making of his art. It is not by accident that the painting that hangs in our bedroom, on the wall we first see on waking in the morning and the last we see before falling off to sleep at night, is one of Sam's magical paintings.

SAM FRANCIS THE MENTOR

Jeff Perkins

I first met Sam Francis in 1963, when I was serving in the United States Air Force in Tokyo. I had known of him since about 1960, when, as an art student in New York City, I saw his painting *Big Red* hanging in the stairway leading up to the main galleries at the Museum of Modern Art, which made a strong impression on me. During basic training in San Antonio, Texas, I had a weekend pass and had read in a local paper that Sam Francis was having a retrospective at the Museum of Modern Art in Houston, Texas, so I took the long bus ride and saw that wonderful exhibition. Eventually I was stationed in Japan and by happenstance I encountered him at an opening in Tokyo. I had also seen his *Tokyo Mural* at the Sogetsu Kai-Kan Hall in Tokyo, when I was participating in Yoko Ono's "Farewell to Tokyo" concert.

When I moved to Los Angeles in 1967 after my service obligation was completed, I was invited to a dinner party for Toshi Ichiyanagi, Yoko's first husband, and Sam was there with his wife, Mako Idemitsu. It was not long after that when I met him again on the projection platform at the Shrine Hall, where I was working with the light show *Single Wing Turquoise Bird*, which was later to come under Sam's generous sponsorship. Sam was attracted to what we were doing in this new medium, supported our work financially, and also facilitated several events and exhibitions for us, which introduced our work to the Los Angeles art community.

It was during this period that Sam received a commission for the largest painting of his career, *Berlin Red*. When he told me of this, I asked if I could film him making the painting. He said that he had never allowed anyone to film him painting before, but he agreed to let me to begin filming him at the Ashland Street studio. My first rolls were shot when he was just finishing up the series called the Edge Paintings. I followed him through the steps in preparation for the painting of *Berlin Red*, which included filming him at work in his first Litho Shop in Santa Monica and then painting *Berlin Red*.

In 1974 I asked Sam if he would agree to a filmed interview with me and, after a certain reluctance, he agreed to do it, once again saying that he didn't very much like interviews about his painting and had never been filmed in such a circumstance. We filmed the interview in his garden at home, which was for me an extraordinary experience. Sam was not an easy interview, but because of my persistence he proved to be generous in unexpected ways. One of Sam's favorite qualities was his elusive wit in certain personal encounters—this was demonstrated (with great challenge to myself) during my interview with him. In 1977 I approached him again, saying that there were certain things that he said during the interview that I wanted him to explain or elaborate upon. He refused to do another interview, but he invited me to film him painting again at the Ashland Street studio, where he was working on two large Matrix Paintings, *Easter* and *Joyous Lake.* Those were the last rolls of film that I shot of Sam.

I always considered my relationship with Sam to be a creative one, an artist-to-artist relationship, and it always remained so. However, because of the nature of our growing friendship, and his influence on me, I began to realize that Sam had become a mentor to me. It was then that I felt that our relationship took on a more formal quality. Sam was a very free person in that he never seemed to express any boundaries either creatively or in personal matters, as was evident in his expansive painting works, or in his ebullient and seductive personality. However, his fierce and compelling devotion to his painting inspired me to have a serious and high regard for the responsibilities that an artist must have in order to produce good works. This also can be considered the responsibility that a mentoring artist must have. Sam was never one to tell another artist what to do; he would simply say if he liked something or not and go on to encourage one to continue the work. Sam was a hardworking artist in the first degree; he was undoubtedly a highly productive artist, as is demonstrated by the vast body of works that he has left for us.

In our personal relationship he influenced me to follow the dictates of my intuition, my soul, and the better part of my nature, and because of his wide and all-encompassing intellect and deep, driving hunger for personal pursuit and excellence, I feel that I could not have found a better influence on my artistic and personal life. I shall never forget him.

SAM FRANCIS (A HAND TO YOUR VISION)

Jerry Aistrip

Yes,
and now besides everything else,
you've gone
and yes,
foundation
I was surprised you made it
this far,
and NO
I'm not ready for you to leave
and no,
I'm not an infantile voice wet with whine,
but met with much regret
more disbelief and a great sorrow
that this world in our lives has come to an end.

Your singular ability to extract the essence
in spoken thought was as direct as a simple
Haiku circle of the East to your vision of
Blue Balls in the West.

Your white hot flesh comet
stone shone sure
and very far.
Your critical mass formed a new
for my sense of values
since our South Dakota September
introduction in 1957.

I came to feel a brotherhood
—sometimes a big-brotherhood—
a sense of alliance and expectation
in the potential for high adventure.
You were a real mentor in my
awareness in a larger world of the
in a larger world of the all possible,
of the ideal.
You had me realize that matters of
great consequence could be
achieved through a flamboyance
of spirit and concept with subtlety
grace and wit.

You had something more: an
intimate contact with the
unconscious through a respect
for dreams: You showed me the
vitality, reflection and the potential
of the dream
Your reality is in the dream
You write your dream
Your dream is becoming to you

Melancholia as a tool
You had TRUTH—like they say—
and STYLE
a few have it
not many get it
but you created it
and it's going to stay here with us
your great GIFT
because of your life
the ecstatic dance of life
behind those eternal BLUE more blue
more blue and all blue eyes
yes.

I suspect you took a great deal with you
I want to say—WAIT A MINUTE
          where's this damned boat going?
          the keel, the oar, the rudder damn it!
          you took it with you!
          but I'm still out here, Goddamn it!
you left a reckless maelstrom
of howling chaos in your
Massive wake, you bastard
but I wouldn't change any thought about you
or any experience with you because behind it all,
you always came with any answer, a vision
and
          HUMOR and LIGHT.
you lived a life of unbounded generosity and
contradiction:
          "Go as far as you can as fast as you can"
          and
          "Try everything once" and
          "There are no problems and no
solutions"
you said it.

Goodbye Sam,
and yes, I see your smile.
and yes, these are tears, and
yes I will paint, play the piano
look at the planet
eat the moment
and think about you.

and Sam, thank you and rest well.

and now it comes down to this:
your departure:
this is what it is
and this is all there is
and what did I expect?
could I have even focused my and
mind to it?
NO.
I would resist the thought that and
this mortal square block of your
soul could come to an end.
would there still be LIGHT
out there after you've left?
or COLOR
or what kind of color now,
Sam

so
here's BLUE for you, Sam,
And color on out—
on out past present and future
speeding beyond thought
all matter
all anything
anywhere.

Oh, Sam is true—
          I know there is
          great evidence to support it—
that you were HERE?
how often you were concealed,
yet you were as present as
air and light from the sun.

PAINT FOR THE PAINTER

Daniel Cytron

I looked around before cleaning up the studio. It was well lit because of a large skylight in the middle of the ceiling. There was a chair, tables, and an area that looked like an old kitchen that you would find in a Masonic lodge. He painted on watercolor paper, large cotton, and linen canvas. He didn't really clean up after himself. He had very fine quality brushes. They were European, not what was sold in Los Angeles in the ordinary art stores. "Pretty exotic!" I said to myself. "This guy is after my own heart."

There were bowls of colored water on the floor and in and on the sink. Paintbrushes with half-hardened paint and evaporated liquid filled the bowls. "These things have been sitting for some time," I said to Ardison. Ardison Phillips had asked me to come with him to work in Sam's studio. Sam sent us to his studio in Ocean Park to move his painting materials from a small inner room into a bigger inner space on the second floor. Richard Diebenkorn also had used these rooms, and we moved his canvases that were still in this room to a new rear studio. In the process of organizing and cleaning, I learned that Sam Francis used oil paint, watercolor, acrylic-oil emulsions, gouache, egg tempera, and water-based acrylic paint. At the end of the day, we constructed a "straw man" out of Sam's painting clothes, hat, and shoes in one corner and organized his new studio with paint, brushes, paper, and small-to-large canvases neatly arranged and ready when he next used the room. That was in 1967; I began as his studio assistant that week.

Years later I went back to school and obtained an additional degree, this time in paint technology. I wanted to know how to make my own paint. With this knowledge, I could also provide Sam with what he needed: colors too expensive and rare for the normal hobbyist manufacturer to sell to the public, and large quantities of those colors in five-gallon containers that were never available to an artist. I could give Sam what he wanted most—quality and exclusivity. My role transformed till we were partners in an enterprise that allowed me to produce colors for my paint and at the same time give Sam a unique palette that other artists could not duplicate.

If there was any person who raised the bar of expectation, it was Sam. "I want the best!" he would say all the time. Our collaboration liberated that quality. I supplied him with watercolors, gouache, acrylic-vinyl paint, egg tempera, oil paint, etching inks, lithographic printing inks, and color dispersions for his oil paintings, monoprints, lithographs, etchings, and water-based paintings on paper and canvas.

I worked with Sam from 1967 until his death. I saw the intensity of his painting, the focus, and the dance that he would do while in the process of painting, printmaking, or drawing. My time with Sam was as his helpmate. I provided those special things that he made into his art. This show is an affirmation of Sam Francis's legacy.

ART IS AT THE HEART OF THE MATTER

Nico Delaive

*E*ight years ago I was first introduced to Sam Francis by one of the artists I represent, Walasse Ting. It was the beginning of a very warm and intense friendship. Every two months I met Sam in California, where he had several studios at the shore in Point Reyes, Palo Alto, and Santa Monica. Sam was a very strong personality, often referred to as "the lion." When looking at him you wouldn't say so, but I've never met anyone so determined in his actions.

He had a passionate poetic mind, revealed in his surroundings and in his sparkling, radiant works of art. Often he wrote to me, and his letters contained beautiful poems. One, which is very typical, often comes into my mind:

Art is at the heart of the matter.

We also had a great deal of fun and good laughs. And that's why I will always remember him and, through his paintings, this thought will be kept alive.

SENSEI, MY FRIEND

Douglas Shields

Of all the varied hats I wore working for Sam, none was more special to me than assisting him in the studio. How many times I'd sit alongside and watch, after opening the paints, laying down sheets of paper or stretched canvases, making sure the water was clean and the spray bottles were full, rollers at the ready, sticks and brushes close by and in abundance. There was no one method of starting. One time Sam would walk around, stirring each color. Another time he would just stare out at the work on the wall, then survey the white surfaces and begin. Sometimes Sam would stand and work, going from one finished white surface to another in the quiet of the evening. Toward the end of his life, he would sit and work surrounded by buckets of liquid paints; bottles of ink, dyes, and watercolors; squeeze bottles of acrylic; and piles of long sticks that to a great extent replaced brushes. It always fascinated me that in a large studio (Sam worked in several with three thousand square feet or more of painting space), we would often end up working in one or another corner almost pinned in by all the buckets of color and tools (Sam's words) that he used to paint with.

How many times Sam would look up at me after spattering a piece of paper with red, green, blue, or purple (the dye colors he called them), spray the color with water, then watch as it spread outward in all directions, and with those intense blue eyes smiling at me, he would say, "I don't know what I'm doing." "Right," I'd reply. Then after a reflective pause he would start adding more and different colors, spatters, and drips. Sometimes he'd wipe up an excessive opaque puddle to bring back a transparent look to the form, maybe a few chosen strokes with a brush. Often he would dip a stick into a bucket, bringing it out loaded with color for "drawing" lines into the image or to just fling it violently down across the surface, pause a little more, then say, "Better not do any more or I'll ruin it." If it was a large sheet of paper, he would help me move it out of the way, having us lift up and go slowly in unison so as not to distort anything. Sam always knew what he was doing. And as for images, he never ran out. Once he told me of an important dream he'd had in which there was a room that only he could open the door to enter and, once inside, he was able to see new images. And this room with its images was only his to visit anytime he wished. Sam often expressed the feeling that there wasn't enough time to paint all the images in his head.

Sam would paint for hours and hours at a time (toward the very end of his life this changed only due to the cancer that sapped his immense energy). I'd watch some, maybe photograph him lay out more paper or canvas; sometimes I had to mix up more color as he worked, fix leaky spray bottles, find that "special" brush, or answer the telephone, which managed to find him no matter where or what he was doing. When he worked on large canvases stapled to the floor, every so often he'd sit on his stool and I'd pull off the paint-soaked socks, spray his feet clean with water, wipe them dry, give him a fresh pair, and send him back to do battle. Usually I ran out of energy before he did.

When Sam was finished for the night, he'd go home for a massage and always ask me to come by in time for a little dinner, that is, after cleaning up the corner he'd been working in and putting tops back on all the opened paints. What a time we had.

These are just a few of the memories I have of working with Sam. I was one of a team (a family in those days) who served him. There were many wonderful times and some not so wonderful. All in all, Sam was my employer, my friend, a brother (he often said he thought of me as a younger brother), and my Sensei. He taught me by example about the nature of pigments and how to use them, and what it means to call oneself a painter.

Sam changed my life forever, down to its very core. He was and is one of the most original modern painters.

APHORISMS

Sam Francis

The eye is the light of the body.

~

Time is the swiftest of all things.

~

I paint time, I am ruin rolled, I am rolled.

~

Color is born of the interpenetration of light and dark.

~

Color is a pattern that plays across the membrane of the mind.

~

Color is a firing of the eye.

~

Color is a series of harmonics everywhere in the universe
being divine whole numbers lasting forever adrift in time.

~

Color is light on fire.

~

Red contains every color even red.

~

All colors in this painting consist of all other colors.

~

These paintings approach you where you are.

~

The space at the center of these paintings is reserved for you.

~

There are as many images as eyes to see.

~

Compensating is the shadow adding to the light what it must at this time.

~

*As you know, energy can have never begun and yet is taken up again and again
and again and lasts forever and forever until it is taken up again.*

~

*Can you unify? Can you unite? Can you bear? Can you bare the weight
at the center? Can you last forever having never begun?*

~

Depth is all.

~

We are always at the center of space.

~

We are always at the center of time.

~

We are always as far as possible from both east and west.

~

We are always as far as possible from earlier and later.

Reprinted from *Saturated Blue: Writings from the Notebooks* (Santa Monica, Calif.: The Lapis
Press, 1995) with permission from the Sam Francis Estate, Los Angeles, California.

Color Plates

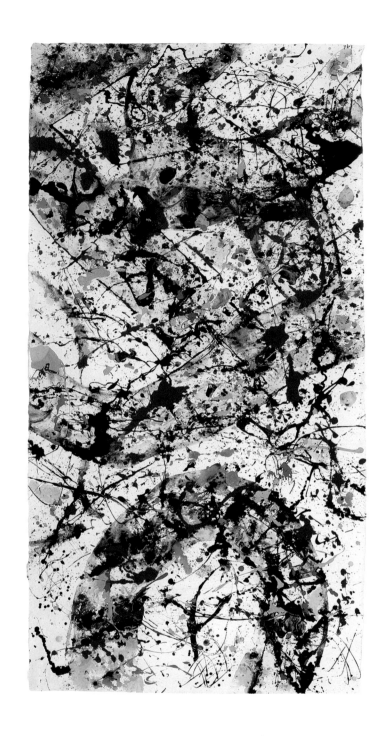

SF 92-111
Untitled
Circa 1992
Acrylic on paper
72" x 36"
Collection: Jessica & Alan Davis, Ventura, Calif.

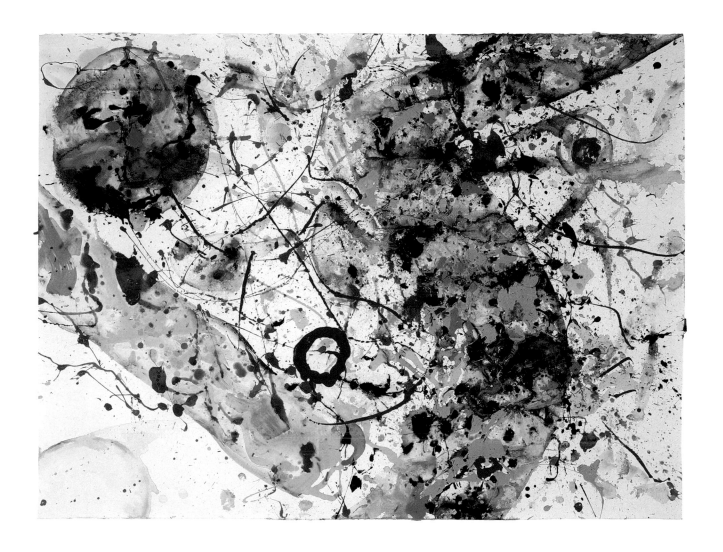

SF 92-112
Untitled
Circa 1992
Acrylic on paper
48" x 64"
Collection: Jessica & Alan Davis, Ventura, Calif.

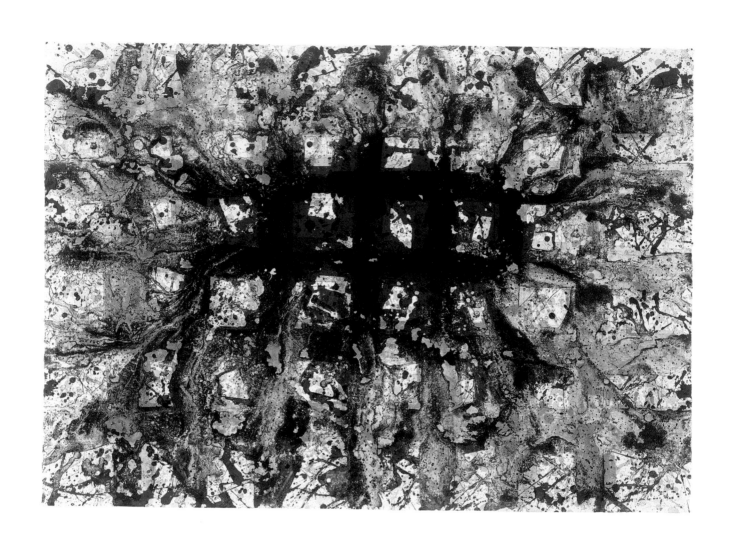

SF 310
Untitled lithograph
1979
Paper: Rives BFK
29.5" x 41.5"
Edition: 30
Collection: Jessica & Alan Davis, Ventura, Calif.

24

SF 324
Untitled lithograph
1975
Paper: Rives BFK
22" x 30"
Edition: 30
Collection: Jessica & Alan Davis, Ventura, Calif.

SF 363
Untitled lithograph
1994
Paper: PTI #112 Waterleaf
23.25" diameter
Edition: 50
Collection: Jessica & Alan Davis, Ventura, Calif.

SFP 88-7
Untitled
Circa 1988
Acrylic on canvas
36" x 48"
Collection: Diane & Daniel Sosin, Las Cruces, N. Mex.

SFP 88-14
Untitled
Circa 1988
Acrylic on canvas
48" x 36"
Collection: Diane & Daniel Sosin, Las Cruces, N. Mex.

28

SF 68-020
Untitled
Circa 1968
Acrylic on paper
40.5" x 27.25"
Collection: Diane & Daniel Sosin, Las Cruces, N. Mex.

SF 255
Untitled lithograph
1979
Paper: Rives BFK
29.5" x 41.5"
Edition: 20
Collection: Diane & Daniel Sosin, Las Cruces, N. Mex.

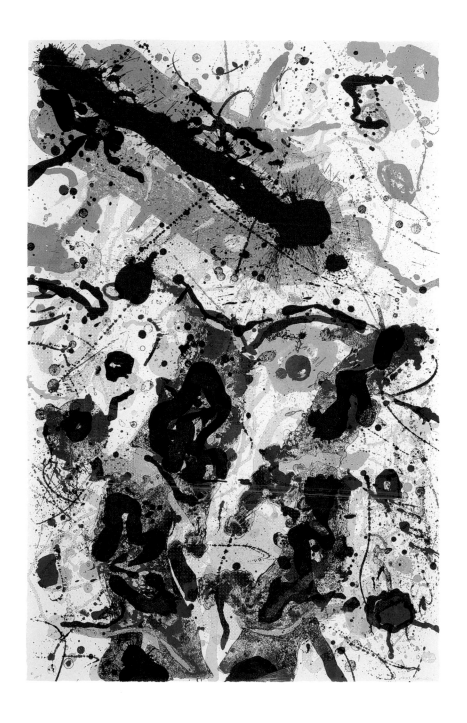

SF 341
Untitled lithograph
1989
Paper: PTI #120 Waterleaf
46.25" x 30"
Edition: 50
Collection: Diane & Daniel Sosin, Las Cruces, N. Mex.

SF 343
Untitled lithograph
1990
Paper: PTI #130 Waterleaf
46" x 30"
Edition: 50
Collection: Diane & Daniel Sosin, Las Cruces, N. Mex.

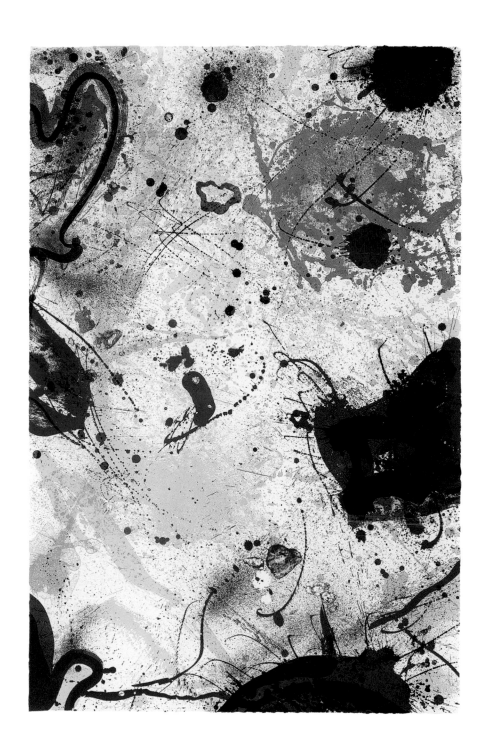

SF 345
Untitled lithograph
1991
Paper: PTI #120 Waterleaf
46.5" x 30"
Edition: 50
Collection: Diane & Daniel Sosin, Las Cruces, N. Mex.

SFP 86-512
Untitled
Circa 1986
Acrylic on canvas
57"x 13"
Collection: Leah & Sam Fischer, Los Angeles

34

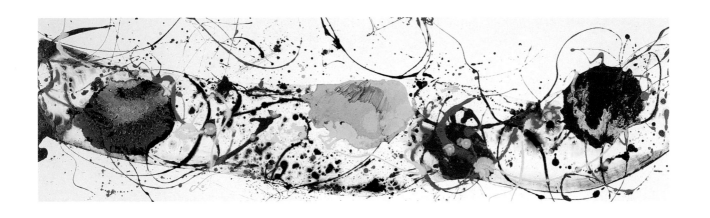

SFP 88-83
Untitled
Circa 1988-89
Acrylic on canvas
36" x 120"
Collection: Leah & Sam Fischer, Los Angeles

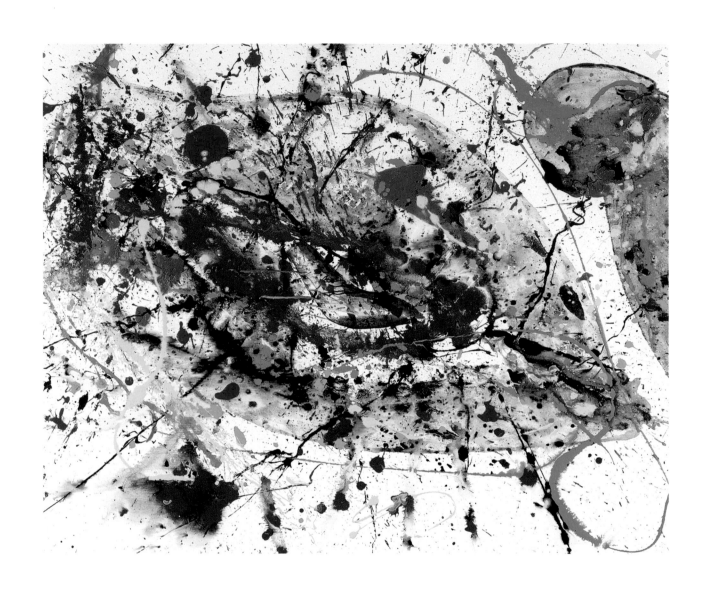

SFP 89-109
Untitled
Circa 1989
Acrylic on canvas
42" x 52"
Collection: Leah & Sam Fischer, Los Angeles

SF 89-205
Untitled
Circa 1989
Acrylic on paper
46" x 60"
Collection: Leah & Sam Fischer, Los Angeles

SFE o88
Untitled etching
1993
Paper: Rives BFK
32" x 43"
Edition: 22
Collection: Leah & Sam Fischer, Los Angeles

SF 259
Untitled lithograph
1980
Paper: Rives BFK
27.5" x 39.25"
Edition: 32
Collection: Leah & Sam Fischer, Los Angeles

SF 319
Untitled lithograph
1987
Paper: Rives BFK
45" x 28"
Edition: 50
Collection: Leah & Sam Fischer, Los Angeles

SF 330
Untitled lithograph
1988
Paper: PTI #120 Waterleaf
44.5" x 29.25"
Edition: 48
Collection: Leah & Sam Fischer, Los Angeles

SF 340
Untitled lithograph
1989
Paper: PTI #120 Waterleaf
45.25" x 29.5"
Edition: 50
Collection: Leah & Sam Fischer, Los Angeles

SF 364
Untitled lithograph
1995
Paper: PTI #112 Waterleaf
49.75" x 31"
Edition: 50
Collection: Leah & Sam Fischer, Los Angeles

SFP 88-272
Untitled
Circa 1988–89
Acrylic on canvas
60" x 36"
Collection: Martin Sosin, Santa Monica, Calif.

44

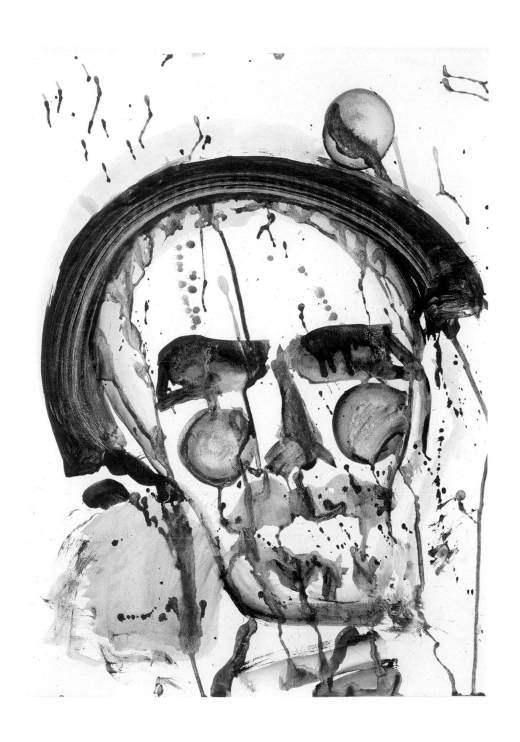

SF 60-1351
Untitled (Self-Portrait)
Circa 1960
Watercolor and gouache on paper
19" x 14"
Collection: Martin Sosin, Santa Monica, Calif.

SFP 79-114
Untitled
Circa 1979
Acrylic on paper
41.25" x 13.5"
Collection: Martin Sosin, Santa Monica, Calif.

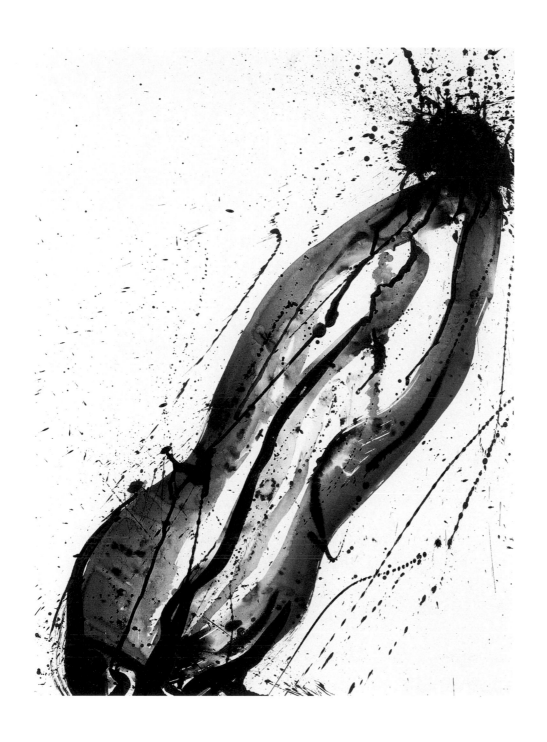

SF 88-459
Untitled
Circa 1988
Acrylic on paper
23.5" x 18"
Collection: Martin Sosin, Santa Monica, Calif.

SF 236
Untitled lithograph
1978
Paper: Rives BFK
38.5" x 28"
Edition: 50
Collection: Martin Sosin, Santa Monica, Calif.

SF 241
Untitled lithograph
1978
Paper: Rives BFK
29.5" x 42"
Edition: 24
Collection: Martin Sosin, Santa Monica, Calif.

SF 267
Untitled lithograph
1982
Paper: Rives BFK
42" x 30"
Edition: 26
Collection: Martin Sosin, Santa Monica, Calif.

SF 342
Untitled lithograph
1990
Paper: PTI #120 Waterleaf
46.5" x 30"
Edition: 10
Collection: Martin Sosin, Santa Monica, Calif.

SF 344
Untitled lithograph
1990
Paper: PTI #120 Waterleaf
46.25" x 30"
Edition: 50
Collection: Martin Sosin, Santa Monica, Calif.

SF 357
Untitled lithograph
1992
Paper: PTI #120 Waterleaf
46.5" x 30"
Edition: 50
Collection: Martin Sosin, Santa Monica, Calif.

SFE 012
Untitled etching
1983
Paper: Somerset Textured White
41.5" x 30.25"
Edition: 50
Collection: Martin Sosin, Santa Monica, Calif.

Key to Paintings and Prints from the Sam Francis Art Collection

Collection	Page	Painting	Page	Print
J. & A. Davis	22	SF 92-111	24	SF 310
	23	SF 92-112	25	SF 324
			26	SF 363
D. & D. Sosin	27	SFP 88-7	30	SF 255
	28	SFP 88-14	31	SF 341
	29	SF 68-020	32	SF 343
			33	SF 345
L. & S. Fischer	34	SFP 86-512	38	SFE 088
	35	SFP 88-83	39	SF 259
	36	SFP 89-109	40	SF 319
	37	SF 89-205	41	SF 330
			42	SF 340
			43	SF 364
M. Sosin	44	SFP 88-272	48	SF 236
	45	SF 60-1351	49	SF 241
	46	SFP 79-114	50	SF 267
	47	SF 88-459	51	SF 342
			52	SF 344
			53	SF 357
			54	SFE 012

CHRONOLOGY OF THE ARTIST (SAM FRANCIS)
AND HIS ALTER EGO (MARTIN SOSIN)
Martin Sosin

	Sam Francis	**Martin Sosin**
Born	June 25, 1923	August 13,1922
Birthplace	San Mateo, California	Brooklyn, New York
Father	Samuel, mathematician	Ralph, pharmacist
Mother	Katherine, piano teacher	Rose, housewife
Sibling	George, born 1926	Jerome, born 1920
Schooling	San Mateo, California	Brooklyn, New York
Higher Education	University of California, Berkeley, 1941–1943	City College of New York, 1940–1942
Military Service	United States Army Air Corps flight training, 1942–1945	United States Army Air Corp, Aerial Mapmaking Wing
Return to University Studies	BA, art, University of California, Berkeley, 1949	BS, accounting, University of California, Los Angeles, 1947
	MA, art history, University of California, Berkeley, 1950	LLD, Southwestern University, 1956

Honors	Honorary PhD, University of California, Berkeley, 1968	Honorary AA degree, Santa Monica College, 2002
	Named "Commandeur de l'ordre des arts et les lettres" by French Minister of Culture Jack Lang, 1983	"Man of the Year Margin of Excellence" award, Santa Monica College, 2002
	"Distinguished Alumnus" award, University of California, Berkeley, 1994	

Marriages, Children	(1) Vera Miller, 1947 Divorced, 1950	(1) Doris Dreller, 1954 Daughter Leah, born 1957 Son Daniel, born 1959 Daughter Jessica, born 1962 Divorced, 1988
	(2) Muriel Goodwin, 1950 Divorced, 1959	
	(3) Teruko Yokoi, 1959 Daughter Kayo, born 1959 Divorced, 1963	(2) Marguerite Holub, 1990 Divorced, 1998
	(4) Masako Idemitsu, 1964 Son Osamu, born 1966 Son Shingo, born 1968 Divorced, 1980	
	(5) Margaret Smith, 1986 Son Augustus, born 1986	

Other

1944	Diagnosed with spinal tuberculosis resulting from an Army Air Corps training accident	
1959	Undergoes successful hernia operation after *Basel* mural falls on him	
1961	Hospitalized in Bern, Switzerland, for tuberculosis of the kidney	
1962	Opens studio at 1378 Main Street, Venice, California	Begins thirty-three-year relationship with Sam as his left-brained alter ego, accountant, lawyer, business manager, and confidant from 1962 to 1994, and also responsible for all of Sam's future corporate organizations

1964	Buys permanent residence at 341-5 West Channel Road, Santa Monica Canyon, California
1968	Moves his studio to 207 Ashland Avenue, Santa Monica, California, sharing space with colleagues
1972	Moves his studio to 1674 20th Street, Santa Monica, California, sets up a lithography section, and hires George Page as master lithographer

1972 Adds large studio to his residence with the help of building contractor Krauth Brand

1973 Forms the Litho Shop, Inc., as business arm with: Sam Francis, President; Martin Sosin, Vice President and Treasurer; George Page, Secretary; and Nancy Mozur, Office Manager and Executive Aide

1974 Moves his studio to 2058 Broadway, Santa Monica, California, and provides Dan Cytron with space to manufacture Sam's special paints

1975 Forms Wind Harvest Company with Bob Thomas as chief engineer and designer of the company's windmills to supply alternative wind energy sources

1976 Commences regular annual one-man exhibitions at Kornfeld and Klipstein Gallery, Bern, Switzerland; Galerie Jean Fournier, Paris; Galerie Delaive, Amsterdam; André Emmerich Gallery, New York; Smith Anderson Gallery, Palo Alto, California; Nicholas Wilder Gallery, Los Angeles; Manny Silverman Gallery, Los Angeles; and Minami Gallery, Tokyo

Diagnosed with coronary heart disease

1976 Michael Blackwood completes sixteen-minute film on Sam Francis.

| 1977 | | Undergoes successful surgery for four bypasses at St. Vincent Hospital in Los Angeles |

1980   Helps organize the Museum of Contemporary Art (MOCA) in Los Angeles. Sits as a founding member of the board of directors and on the architecture committee. Instrumental in getting Pontus Hulten as the founding artistic director and Arata Isuzaki as the architect for the permanent building on Grand Avenue in Los Angeles.

1982   Installs etching studio at the Litho Shop studio with Jacob Samuel as master etcher

1984   Forms the Lapis Press with the purpose of publishing timely and unusual scholarly texts and hires Robert Shapazian as the executive director

Forms a homeopathic medicine business, NATRX, with Robert Jacobs in Santa Monica, California

1987   Forms the Sam Francis Medical Research Center, Inc. (SFMRCI), a tax-exempt corporation for naturopathic alternative medical research and studies on environmental and communicative diseases

1990   Forms the Sam Francis Art Museum, Inc. (SFAMI), a tax-exempt corporation to support charitable donations, perpetuate his artistic legacy, and be the main recipient of his estate

Leases large studio at 589 North Venice Boulevard, Venice, California, which also houses the Lapis Press

Diagnosed with prostate cancer and relies solely on alternative treatments for the disease   Diagnosed with prostate cancer

1991		Commences radiation treatment at UCLA Medical Center in Los Angeles; the cancer goes into remission

1992 Publishes *The Prints of Sam Francis: A Catalogue Raisonné, 1960–1990,* by Connie Lembark

Sam gives him a copy of the catalogue raisonné, inscribing it:

> For Marty
>   Who is always next to me
>   on the side of my heart.
>   Love
>   Sam

1993 Pontus Hulten, director of the Kunst-Und Ausstellungshalle der Bundesrenoublik Deutschland in Bonn, Germany, organizes a retrospective of Sam's work, February 12 to April 4

Together with SFAMI, makes a gift of ten paintings covering the major portions of his body of work to MOCA

On October 8, as Sam's alter ego in his absence due to illness, gives a speech at the Museum of Contemporary Art dinner honoring Sam for his gift of ten paintings

1994 Receives the first "Distinguished Alumnus" award from the University of California, Berkeley, Art Practices Department, at a dinner at the Berkeley Art Museum on October 7, which he could not attend because of illness. The dinner included an exhibition of the many paintings that he gave his alma mater over the years.

With SFAMI, completes the creation of the Sam Francis Graduate Student Endowed Fellowship, a $150,000 endowment to support promising graduate students in fine arts

Dies of prostate cancer on November 4

And also on November 4, Marty's persona as "Sam's alter ego" ended.

But at the same time, as he had promised Sam, Marty would do all he could to disseminate Sam's legacy as the seminal abstract impressionist artist of the twentieth century.

Notes on Contributors

Jerry Aistrip (Los Angeles) was a studio assistant, gallery exhibition coordinator, and friend of Sam.

Daniel Cytron (Los Angeles) was a colleague, a chemist, the manufacturer of all of Sam's special paints, and his friend.

Nico Delaive (Amsterdam), an art dealer for many years in the Netherlands, was a friend of Sam.

André Emmerich (New York) was a New York City art dealer for many years and a lifelong friend of Sam.

Nancy Mozur (Santa Monica, California) worked with Sam for many years, ran his Litho Shop activities from 1973 to 1989, and created the overall cataloguing of Sam's works of art.

George Page (Little Rock, California) worked with Sam as his lithographer from 1973 to 1994 and was an officer in all of Sam's corporate entities and a lifelong friend.

Jeff Perkins (New York), a photographer and the producer of the film *Sam Francis*, was a friend of Sam since 1976.

Robert Shapazian (Los Angeles) was the director of the Lapis Press, created by Sam Francis as a wholly owned subsidiary of the Litho Shop. He took his doctorate at Harvard University and is currently the director of the Gagosian Art Gallery in Beverly Hills, California.

Douglas Shields (Inverness, California) received a BFA degree from Chouinard Art Institute in Los Angeles in 1972, after which he began a long career as Sam's studio aide, close friend, and confidant from 1978 to 1994.

Martin Sosin (Santa Monica, California) represented Sam as a certified public accountant and lawyer from 1962 to 1994, during which time he was responsible for all of Sam's business activities and the creation of the Litho Shop (1973), the Lapis Press (1984), the Sam Francis Medical Research Center (1987), the Sam Francis Art Museum (1990), and the Sam Francis Graduate Student Endowment at University of California, Berkeley (1994).

Partial List of Museum Exhibitions

Art Institute, Chicago

Colorado State University Museum, Fort Collins, Colorado

Toyama Museum, Tokyo

Museum of Modern Art, Tokyo

Ohara Museum of Art, Murashiki, Japan

Museum Van Der Togi, Amsterdam

Museum of Contemporary Art, Los Angeles

Museum of Modem Art, New York

Pasadena Art Museum, Pasadena, California

San Francisco Art Museum, San Francisco

Modera Museet, Stockholm

Museum of Fine Art, Houston

University Art Museum, Berkeley, California

Centre National d'Art Contemporain, Paris

Musée d'Art Moderne, Paris

Institute of Contemporary Art, London

Art Institute of Chicago, Chicago

Kunsthalle, Bern, Switzerland

Museum of Fine Art, Pittsburgh

Los Angeles County Museum of Art, Los Angeles

Whitney Museum of American Art, New York

Dallas Museum of Fine Art, Dallas, Texas

Oakland Museum of Art, Oakland, California

Stanford University Museum of Art, Palo Alto, California

Idemitsu Art Museum, Tokyo

Louisiana Museum of Art, Humlebaek, Denmark

Centre Pompidou, Paris

Liljevalchs Konsthall, Stockholm

Otis Art Institute, Los Angeles

Institute of Contemporary Art, Boston

Israel Museum, Jerusalem

Corcoran Gallery of Art, Washington, DC

Albright-Knox Art Gallery, Buffalo, New York

Walker Art Center, Minneapolis

Partial List of Gallery Exhibitions

Ace Gallery, Los Angeles
Ruth Schaffner Gallery, Santa Barbara, California
Faith and Charity in Hope Gallery, Hope, Idaho
Mantenshi Gallery, Tokyo
Foundation Maeght, St. Paul, France
Studio Marcon, Milan, Italy
Art Attack Gallery, Boise, Idaho
John Berggruen Gallery, San Francisco, California
Pamela Auchincloss Gallery, Santa Barbara, California
Cantor/Lemberg Gallery, Birmingham, Michigan
Robert Elkon Gallery, New York
Thomas Babeor Gallery, La Jolla, California
Knoedler Gallery, London, England
Stephen Wirtz Gallery, San Francisco
Hokin Gallery, Bay Harbor, Florida
Angles Gallery, Santa Monica, California
Heland Thorden Wetterling Gallery, Stockholm, Sweden
G. Dalsheimer Gallery, Baltimore, Maryland
Galeria Eude, Barcelona, Spain
Manny Silverman Gallery, Los Angeles
Galerie Pudelko, Bonn, West Germany
Lever/Meyerson Galleries, New York
Greenberg Gallery, St. Louis, Missouri
Galerie De Seoul, Seoul
Bernard Jacobson Gallery, London
Sun Valley Center Gallery, Ketchum, Idaho
Linda Farris Gallery, Seattle, Washington
Gallery Delaive, Amsterdam
Ogawa Art Foundation, Tokyo
Ochi Gallery, Sun Valley, Idaho
Talbot Rice Gallery, New York
Gagosian Gallery, New York
Galerie Daniel Papierski, Paris
Kukje Gallery, Seoul

Bobby Greenfield Fine Art Gallery, Venice, California

Michele Cohen Gallery, New York

Galerie Baukust, Cologne, Germany

Daco Verlag, Stuttgart, Germany

Galerie Du Dracon, Paris

Martha Jackson Gallery, New York

Kornfeld and Klipstein Gallery, Bern, Switzerland

Esther Bear Gallery, Santa Barbara, California

Minami Gallery, Tokyo

Pierre Matisse Gallery, New York

Galerie Rive Droite, Paris

Hyakksten Tokyo Department Store, Tokyo

Kintetsu Department Store, Osaka, Japan

Gimpels, FLS, Ltd., London

Kornfeld Gallery, Bern, Switzerland

Galerie du Dragon, Paris

Studio Paul Facchetti, Paris

Galleria di Spazio, Rome

Galerie Arnaud, Paris

Arts Council Gallery, Cambridge, England

Zoe Dosanne Gallery, Seattle

Felix Landau Gallery, Los Angeles

André Emmerich Gallery, New York

Nicholas Wilder Gallery, Los Angeles

Galerie Jean Fournier, Paris

Richard Gray Gallery, Chicago

Smith Anderson Gallery, Palo Alto, California

Brooke Alexander Gallery, New York